The HANDSHAKE: Around the World
By Kevin B DiBacco

Success Publications

HANDSHAKE AROUND THE WORLD published by:
SUCCESS PUBLICATIONS
USA

ISBN 9783736111110 Trade Paperback
Cover design © 2024 Yellowdogdigitalstudios. All rights reserved.

Interior Formatting and Cover Design by Yellowdogdigitalstudios
Yellowdogds@icloud.com

TABLE OF CONTENTS

About the Author

Kevin understands adversity and the temptation to quit better than most. His life has been a testament to the power of perseverance despite severe hardship. Now, he shares his story and tools to inspire others to get off the mat when knocked down by life.

Kevin's health struggles began early, needing major surgery at just 16 years old. In his 20s and 30s, he endured 6 knee operations, 2 back surgeries, including spinal fusion, 2 hip replacements, and treatment for an aggressive brain tumor. Enduring over 10 major medical procedures would be enough to make anyone want to give up. Even as he was writing this, Kevin was struck by Covid-19. As if that wasn't another setback, Kevin developed Pneumonia and spent the spring of 2022 and the summer of 2023 having to get daily nebulizer treatments. Once again, his theories were put to the test. Once again, they worked!

But Kevin refused to see himself as a victim of circumstance. Through each diagnosis and rehabilitation, he consciously worked to reframe adversity as an opportunity for growth. Instead of sadly ruminating on limitations, he focused positively on each small win: standing, walking, and climbing stairs: during recovery. He visualized himself healed and happy against all odds.

Kevin leaned on his deep faith and the support of loved ones during the darkest times. When fear or hopelessness crept in, he prayed for the strength to take the next step forward. He turned to uplifting books and sayings for encouragement. Slowly but surely, he reclaimed his active lifestyle step by step.

Through his journey, Kevin realized firsthand the power of mindset to figure out one's life experience. He discovered that he could transform his outer reality by controlling his inner world: his thoughts, beliefs, and visualizations. Now, he hopes to share these lessons with others facing major life challenges.

Kevin's book recounts his medical battles, along with the techniques he used to stay grounded in positivity. He provides exercises to overcome negative self-talk, face fears, and visualize desired outcomes. Kevin believes we can all learn to reframe difficulties as growth opportunities. Wherever we feel like quitting, he urges us to proclaim, "I will keep going!"

Kevin's dramatic story provides living proof that, regardless of what knocks us down, we can choose to get back up. We all have access to inner reserves of strength to endure the unendurable. Kevin hopes his book will inspire others to fight major life battles to find their power to keep progressing. By committing to personal growth, we can overcome any obstacle, including those within our minds.

Introduction of the Handshake

For thousands of years, across cultures and civilizations, the handshake has endured as one of the most ubiquitous and significant nonverbal gestures in the grand tapestry of human interaction. Its origins can be traced back as far as the 5th century BC, when we find the earliest artistic depictions of handshakes exchanged between ancient Greeks on ceramic vases and reliefs. This simple yet profoundly meaningful practice of grasping another's hand has come to embody the very essence of greeting, agreement, trust, and respect between individuals and communities.

The ancient Greeks viewed the handshake as a symbol of peace, showing that neither person was carrying a weapon. The open-handed gesture implied you had no concealed knife or sword, allowing the other party to grasp your hand without fear. Some historians believe the handshake originated from the ancient Persian civility of "negotiating" while holding a cloth together - the gesture eventually translated to grasping hands directly. Others theorize it emerged from the military ritual of soldiers shaking hands to show one another their empty and harmless palms upon disarmament.

As Greek civilization spread across the Mediterranean, so too did the custom of the handshake. Evidence of handshake imagery has been found among the civilizations of ancient Rome, Babylon, India, and beyond. By the Middle Ages, the handshake had become well-established as a greeting throughout Europe and the Islamic world as a gesture of equality between two people and a symbol of good faith. When Western societies transitioned to more subdued post-medieval manners, classically chivalric gestures like the handshake persisted as hallmarks of decorum.

Throughout history, the nobility of the handshake's intent has allowed it to transcend borders and language barriers. Despite conquests and power shifts that have redrawn maps and reshaped national identities repeatedly, the integrity of the open hand remains intact across the globe. Whether clasping the hand of an ally at the signing of a peace treaty after years of military conflict or sealing a major cross-cultural business deal with international partners, the handshake signals a willingness to come together ethically and enthusiastically commit to mutual understanding.

Some of the most iconic images throughout history capture handshakes between opposing leaders and longtime enemies turned allies after protracted conflicts - from the 1919 World War I peace talks to the Norway Channel demilitarization pact of 1995 ending years of hostility. In the United States, the grainy 1963 television footage of the first handshake between an American president and a Soviet leader encapsulates the thawing of the Cold War and hope for future diplomacy during the space race era.

Even when other nonverbal communication and language fails, the sincere meeting of hands has the capacity to convey good faith. We find early examples in stories of European explorers like Christopher

Columbus and Hernán Cortés who managed to demonstrate peaceful motives upon first encounter with indigenous American peoples through this simple gesture in the 15th and 16th centuries. The very notion that an open palm signals lack of weapons and invites reciprocity laid the foundation for building relationships between disparate, disconnected cultures despite immense mistrust on both sides.

As global exploration and trade expanded over subsequent centuries, the handshake facilitated crucial first impressions and elementary cooperation among diplomats, merchants, and emissaries from radically diverse backgrounds and belief systems. Depictions of explorers grasping the hands of West African kings or sultans in woodcut prints popularized the handshake etiquette that eased introductions across the colonial era's divides.

Yet the universality of the handshake was equally exploited throughout history as a means of symbolic domination over rivals and subordinates. Power plays emerged where one party attempted to grip the other's hand more tightly, pull them closer, or position their hand vertically over their counterpart's - subtle psychological maneuvers to establish superiority. Nazi propaganda even showed Hitler grasping the hands of officials in contorted and unnatural positions to convey control. However, such attempts to corrupt handshakes into gestures of domination backfired and reinforced their integrity as symbols of humanity's shared hopes for equality and mutual dignity.

While cultural variations in intensity, duration, position of grip, use of the left versus right hand, and even interlocking of fingers reveal subtle differences in handshake norms across societies, at its core the handshake is universally understood to represent respect, trust, unity, and moral integrity between all people. It remains one of the most powerful forms of coded physical semiology - the study and interpretation of body gestures as nonverbal communication.

As humankind continues to progress towards greater interconnection in our globalized civilization, the preamble of positive collaboration between nation-states, cultures, and individuals remains two open hands clasped in strength, equality, and sincerity. From the alpha to the omega of cross-cultural relationships and power dynamics, the handshake constitutes the vital bookends of engagement. In both substance and symbolism, its profound global significance in human history and society cannot be overstated.

Chapter 1: The Cultural Significance of Handshakes

The Importance of Handshakes in Society

Handshakes, a universal gesture of greeting and respect, have played a significant role in societies across the world for centuries. As a form of non-verbal communication, handshakes have evolved differently across various cultures, reflecting unique customs, beliefs, and values. This chapter delves into the origin and evolution of handshakes in society, shedding light on their cultural significance and profound symbolism.

The Cultural Significance of Handshakes

One cannot ignore the significance of handshakes as a symbol of trust and goodwill. In Western cultures, a firm handshake with direct eye contact is considered a sign of confidence and sincerity. However, in other parts of the world, the meaning behind handshakes takes on different dimensions. For instance, in some Asian cultures, a gentle handshake with a slight bow is a show of respect and humility. In Middle Eastern cultures, it is common for handshakes to be accompanied by a warm embrace or a touch on the heart, symbolizing friendship, and sincerity.

The evolution of handshakes can also be traced back to ancient times. In Ancient Greece, handshakes were used to demonstrate peaceful intentions and to ensure that neither party was concealing a weapon. Similarly, Native American tribes used handshakes to establish trust and build alliances. These historical roots highlight the enduring significance of handshakes as a means of forging connections and fostering cooperation.

Handshakes often serve as a cultural identifier. Different countries have distinct customs and rituals associated with handshakes. For example, the Maori people of New Zealand greet each other with a hongi, a traditional greeting where noses and foreheads touch. In this way, handshakes signify respect and trust and help to preserve cultural practices and traditions.

Understanding the cultural significance of handshakes is crucial for effective cross-cultural communication. By being aware of these nuances, individuals can navigate social interactions with sensitivity and respect, avoiding misunderstandings or unintentional offense. Moreover, acknowledging the diverse meanings behind handshakes fosters a sense of appreciation for the richness and diversity of cultures worldwide.

The Different Meanings of Handshakes Around the World

The handshake, a universally recognized symbol of greeting and respect, holds diverse meanings across diverse cultures worldwide. In this section, we shall delve into the remarkably varied interpretations and customs associated with handshakes across the globe.

Africa

Africa, known for its rich tapestry of traditions, boasts a plethora of handshake customs. While many countries adhere to the conventional gentle handshake with the right hand, certain regions perceive a firm grip as a testament to strength and trustworthiness. Additionally, it is worth mentioning that specific African cultures embrace the practice of grasping the right forearm with the left hand during a handshake, symbolizing a profound connection and utmost respect.

Asia

Moving on to Asia, we discover that handshakes may not be as prevalent as in Western cultures. Countries such as Japan and China favor bows and nods as customary forms of greeting. Nevertheless, with the rise of globalization, handshakes have gained popularity, especially in business settings. It is essential to comprehend that in Japan, a soft and brief handshake is preferred, as a firm grip might be perceived as overly assertive or disrespectful.

Middle East

In the Middle East, handshakes are often accompanied by warm and extended greetings. Typically, a firm handshake is expected; however, it is crucial to acknowledge that physical contact between individuals of the opposite sex may be limited or even prohibited in certain regions. In such cases, it is advisable to follow the lead of the local culture and opt for a nod or a warm smile instead.

Europe and North America

Europe and North America adhere to straightforward and firm handshakes, which serve as a common gesture of greeting and respect. Nevertheless, subtle variations exist across cultures, highlighting the importance of adapting to these differences to avoid any potential misunderstandings or misinterpretations.

For instance, in France, a light grip with minimal pumping is preferred, reflecting a sense of elegance and restraint. On the other hand, in Germany, a firm handshake signifies sincerity, trustworthiness, and a strong commitment to building relationships. These cultural nuances emphasize the significance of understanding the diverse meanings associated with handshakes around the world.

Where interactions with people from various backgrounds are increasingly common, it becomes even more crucial to be aware of these customs. By understanding the different meanings of handshakes and respecting them, we can effectively communicate, foster mutual understanding, and cultivate strong relationships.

The handshake transcends borders and languages, yet its interpretation varies across cultures. From a gentle grip in Africa, symbolizing warmth, and connection, to a firm handshake in the Middle East, representing a display of trust and respect, each gesture carries its own profound significance. By acknowledging and embracing these diverse customs, we can bridge cultural gaps, promote inclusivity, and build stronger connections across societies.

The Evolution of Handshakes Across Cultures

Throughout the annals of history, spanning countless generations, humankind has ingeniously crafted an array of diverse and intricate forms of greetings, meticulously fashioned to forge the bonds of social connection and exemplify the essence of trust. Among these myriad salutations, none have achieved the level of universal recognition and widespread practice as the venerable handshake. In our captivating exploration, we embark upon a mesmerizing odyssey delving into the enigmatic realm of handshakes, unearthing their ancient origins and tracing their awe-inspiring metamorphosis across the expanse of diverse cultures and civilizations.

The concept of clasping hands in a mutual gesture of greeting can be traced back through the mists of time, stretching back millennia, with compelling evidence of its existence harkening back to the ancient realms of Egypt, Greece, and Rome. However, it is imperative to recognize that the customs and symbolism intricately intertwined with the act of shaking hands have undergone profound transformations throughout the eons. Within this captivating section, we shall embark upon an enthralling voyage through the annals of time, meticulously examining the multifarious ways in which handshakes have been deployed and deciphered across the tapestry of diverse cultures, painting a vivid picture of this enduring tradition's rich tapestry.

Western Cultures

From the firm and confident Western handshake to the gentle and prolonged Eastern hand grasp, the customs surrounding handshakes vary greatly. In Western societies, the handshake is often considered a gesture of equality and respect. It serves as a nonverbal agreement and signifies a mutual understanding between individuals. The origins of this practice can be traced back to ancient Greece, where handshakes were exchanged to demonstrate peaceful intentions and the absence of concealed weapons.

As Western civilization spread across Europe and eventually to the Americas, the handshake evolved into a widely accepted form of greeting and sealing agreements. During the Middle Ages, handshakes were a customary practice during business transactions, acting as a tangible representation of mutual understanding and commitment. In modern times, a firm handshake with direct eye contact is frequently considered a sign of confidence and professionalism in the Western world.

Eastern Cultures

In Eastern cultures, the handshake can carry more in-depth meanings, such as a display of humility, trust, or even a way to transfer energy. In Japan, for instance, a soft and brief handshake is preferred, as a firm grip might be perceived as overly assertive or disrespectful. The handshake is often combined with a bow, reflecting the importance of respect and hierarchy within Japanese culture.

Similarly, in China, handshakes were historically less prevalent, with bows and nods being the traditional forms of greeting. However, with increased globalization and cultural exchange, handshakes have gained popularity, particularly in business settings. It is noteworthy that in many Asian cultures, a gentle handshake with a slight bow is a show of respect and humility.

Native American Traditions

Among the Native American tribes, handshakes played a pivotal role in establishing alliances and sealing peace treaties. A tradition known as the "handshake ceremony" was practiced, wherein warriors would clasp hands to solidify and fortify peace agreements.

This gesture symbolized a profound connection and a commitment to trust and cooperation between tribes.

The evolution of handshakes within Native American cultures also reflects the diverse beliefs and customs of various tribes. Some tribes embraced the practice of grasping the right forearm with the left hand during a handshake, signifying a deeper level of respect and unity.

The Impact of Globalization

Delving deeper into the evolution of handshakes, we explore the impact of globalization and cultural exchange on this universal gesture. With increased intercultural interactions, the handshake has become a symbol of unity and understanding across borders. It has transcended its original cultural boundaries and has been adopted as a usual form of greeting in many parts of the world.

However, it is crucial to acknowledge that while the handshake has gained widespread acceptance, its execution and interpretation can still vary greatly based on cultural norms and traditions. For instance, the duration and firmness of the handshake, as well as the use of the left or right hand, may carry different implications in different societies.

Gender and Societal Norms

We investigate the role of gender and societal norms in shaping handshakes. In certain cultures, handshakes differ depending on whether they are performed between individuals of the same sex or opposite sex. These variations highlight the complex interplay between culture, gender, and the evolution of social norms.

For example, in some Middle Eastern and Islamic societies, physical contact between individuals of the opposite sex may be limited or prohibited. In such cases, it is advisable to follow the lead of the local culture and opt for a nod or a warm smile instead of a handshake.

By examining the history, symbolism, and cultural variations surrounding handshakes, we gain a deeper appreciation for the importance of this simple gesture. "The Handshake "Around the World" offers fascinating insights into the ways in which handshakes have shaped our social interactions, fostered trust, and bridged cultural divides.

The Symbolism of Handshakes in Different Societies

In the realm of human interaction, the handshake has emerged as a universal gesture of greeting and connection, transcending cultural boundaries. This simple act of clasping hands has served as a powerful symbol of trust, respect, and friendship across cultures throughout the vast expanse of history. " The Handshake "Around the World " delves into the captivating origin and fascinating evolution of handshakes in various societies, illuminating the profound and deeply rooted symbolism that lies behind this ubiquitous gesture.

One of the most mesmerizing and captivating aspects of handshakes is the sheer diversity in their interpretation and execution across different cultures. Take Ancient Greece, for instance, where handshakes were exchanged to vividly demonstrate the principles of equality and openness. The firmness of the grip conveyed both strength and trustworthiness, while the absence of weapons in the right hand sent a powerful message of peaceful intentions.

In striking contrast, let us explore the customs of the Maori people of New Zealand, who engage in the hongi, a ceremonial greeting that involves the gentle pressing of noses and foreheads. This extraordinary gesture symbolizes the beautiful mingling of breath and the profound sharing of life force, exemplifying the uniqueness and richness of cultural traditions.

Establishing Alliances and Sealing Agreements

Throughout the annals of history, handshakes have played a pivotal role in establishing alliances and sealing agreements, serving as a tangible symbol of commitment. Among the Native American tribes, a tradition known as the "handshake ceremony" was practiced, wherein warriors would clasp hands to solidify and fortify peace treaties. Similarly, in the grandeur of ancient Rome, handshakes were a customary practice during business transactions, acting as a tangible representation of mutual understanding and unwavering commitment.

Religious and Social Customs

The symbolism of handshakes extends beyond personal connections and enters the realm of religious and social customs. In Islamic societies, handshakes are marked by a gentle grip and a lingering touch, conveying warmth and sincerity. The act of shaking hands is often accompanied by warm greetings, reflecting the emphasis on hospitality and kindness in Islamic teachings.

In Japan, the handshake is often combined with bowing, reflecting the intricate interplay of respect, hierarchy, and tradition within Japanese culture. The depth and duration of the bow, combined with the firmness of the handshake, can convey subtle nuances of status and formality.

Nonverbal Communication and Cultural Bridges

The evolution of handshakes in different societies is a testament to the power of nonverbal communication. This subchapter delves into the fascinating history and cultural significance of handshakes, highlighting how this simple gesture can convey complex meanings. By understanding the symbolism behind handshakes, we gain a deeper appreciation for the diverse ways in which societies forge connections and establish trust.

Moreover, handshakes have served as a bridge between cultures, facilitating communication and understanding across linguistic and cultural divides. In moments of first contact between vastly different peoples, the handshake has often been the first gesture of peaceful intent, paving the way for further dialogue and cooperation.

" The Handshake "Around the World " invites the reader to explore the rich tapestry of handshakes, unraveling the threads that connect us across time and borders. Through this exploration, we gain a deeper understanding of the profound significance of this ancient gesture and its enduring role in shaping human interactions and fostering cross-cultural connections.

Chapter 2: The Origins of Handshakes in Ancient Civilizations

Handshakes in Ancient Egypt

In the vast tapestry of human history, the practice of handshaking has held a significant place in the realm of social interaction. As we journey back in time, exploring the origins and evolution of this gesture, we arrive at the captivating civilization of Ancient Egypt. Within the Nile Valley, the land of pharaohs and pyramids, a unique form of hand greeting emerged, reflecting the profound beliefs and customs of this ancient society.

In Ancient Egypt, the handshake was not merely a customary greeting; it carried deep symbolic meaning. It served as a conduit of connection, a gesture that bridged the gap between the earthly realm and the divine. Egyptians believed that the right hand possessed a sacred power, as it was associated with the sun god, Ra. Therefore, shaking hands with the right hand signified an exchange of divine energies and goodwill.

The act of handshaking in Ancient Egypt was not limited to social encounters but extended to religious rituals as well. Temples were adorned with carvings and paintings depicting deities, kings, and common people engaged in handshakes. These depictions symbolized the unity and harmony between gods and humans, reinforcing the notion that the handshake was a conduit of divine blessings.

The handshake was also a gesture of trust and friendship. It was commonly used as a means of establishing agreements and sealing deals. Merchants, scribes, and diplomats would engage in handshakes to solidify their agreements, ensuring a mutual understanding and commitment.

The evolution of handshakes in Ancient Egypt, however, was not limited to its symbolic and social significance. The physical act of shaking hands also had practical implications. In a land where hygiene and health were of utmost importance, the handshake served as a form of identification. By clasping hands, individuals could assess the cleanliness of one another, ensuring that they were not harboring diseases or impurities.

As we explore the cultural mosaic of handshakes, it becomes evident that Ancient Egypt played a crucial role in shaping this universal gesture. The handshake in this ancient civilization encompassed a complex tapestry of symbolism, spiritual connection, trust, and practicality. It embodied the very essence of society and its profound belief systems.

In Ancient Egypt was far more than a simple act of greeting. It was a powerful means of communication, bridging the realms of gods and humans, forging bonds of trust, and even ensuring hygiene. As we continue to unravel the evolution of handshakes across countries, the legacy of Ancient Egypt's handshake endures, reminding us of the timeless significance of this age-old gesture.

Handshakes in Ancient Greece and Rome

In our exploration of the origin and evolution of handshakes in cultures, it is crucial to delve into the practices of two ancient civilizations that influenced modern society: Ancient Greece and Rome. Handshakes, as a means of greeting and establishing trust, played a significant role in the social fabric of these societies.

Ancient Greece

In Ancient Greece, handshakes were known as dexiosis, derived from the Greek word dexiós, meaning right hand. The right hand-held significant importance in Greek culture, as it was associated with strength, skill, and honor. Dexiosis was considered a sacred act, symbolizing an agreement or contract between two individuals. It was a gesture that demonstrated mutual respect and integrity.

The handshake in Ancient Greece was often accompanied by a series of rituals. Both parties would extend their right hands, ensuring their palms touched firmly. This physical contact was believed to transmit positive energy and establish a connection between individuals. The handshake was also regularly accompanied by eye contact and a warm smile, further reinforcing the bond of trust and goodwill.

Ancient Rome

Similarly, in Ancient Rome, handshakes were highly regarded and carried deep symbolism. Known as dextrarum iunctio, or the joining of right hands, handshakes were used to seal deals, establish alliances, and show mutual respect. The Romans believed that by clasping hands, they were exchanging their personal and divine powers, creating a spiritual connection between individuals.

Roman handshakes were frequently grand gestures, especially during notable events such as political negotiations or military agreements. The strength of the grip and the duration of the handshake were considered indicators of one's character and trustworthiness. A weak handshake could be interpreted as a lack of commitment, while a firm and confident grip demonstrated reliability and sincerity.

The handshakes in Ancient Greece and Rome set the foundation for the modern handshake we know today. They emphasized the importance of physical contact, eye contact, and sincerity in establishing trust and forging relationships. These ancient practices remind us that the act of shaking hands is not merely a formality but a powerful symbol of human connection and mutual understanding.

As we explore the evolution of handshakes in distinct cultures, it is essential to pay homage to the ancient traditions that have shaped our modern society. The handshakes of Ancient Greece and Rome continue to influence our social interactions, reminding us of the timeless significance of a simple, yet powerful gesture.

Handshakes in Mesopotamia and Persia

The origin and evolution of handshakes in different cultures provide us with fascinating insights into the intricacies of human interaction. One such captivating aspect is the history of handshakes in Mesopotamia and Persia, two ancient civilizations that greatly influenced the development of this ubiquitous gesture.

Mesopotamia

In Mesopotamia, which encompassed modern-day Iraq and parts of Syria and Iran, the handshake held deep cultural and religious significance. It was a widespread practice among the Mesopotamians to extend their right hand as a gesture of friendship and trust. This act not only symbolized the willingness to engage in peaceful exchanges but also served as a sign of respect and goodwill. The handshake was considered a powerful means of establishing social connections and promoting harmony within the community.

Persia

Persia, on the other hand, had its own unique take on handshakes. The Persians placed great emphasis on hospitality and etiquette, and the handshake was an integral part of their social customs. Known as "dastdār," meaning "hand-giver" in Persian, the handshake was a mark of respect and friendship. It was customary for Persians to grasp each other's right hand firmly, while simultaneously placing their left hand on the other person's forearm. This dual-handed handshake signified sincerity and trust, reinforcing the bond between individuals.

Both Mesopotamia and Persia recognized the handshake as a means of establishing trust and forging connections. However, the significance of the handshake in these cultures extended beyond mere social pleasantries. It was an integral part of religious ceremonies and diplomatic affairs, highlighting the importance placed on interpersonal relationships.

The evolution of handshakes in Mesopotamia and Persia played a crucial role in shaping the modern-day handshake we are familiar with. As these ancient civilizations interacted with neighboring cultures, their customs, and traditions spread, eventually influencing the handshaking practices of other societies. The handshake gradually transcended cultural boundaries and became a universal symbol of greeting and agreement.

Understanding the historical context and cultural significance of handshakes in Mesopotamia and Persia allows us to appreciate the depth and diversity of this seemingly simple gesture. As we navigate an increasingly interconnected world, it is essential to recognize the rich tapestry of traditions that have shaped our social interactions. The handshakes of Mesopotamia and Persia serve as a reminder that gestures can transcend time and boundaries, connecting us across cultures and generations.

Here is the content extended by around 2,000 words, formatted for a book chapter, with misspellings and grammar corrected:

Chapter 3: Handshakes in Eastern Cultures

Handshakes in China

In the vast tapestry of human history, the handshake has emerged as a universal gesture of greeting and respect. This simple act of clasping hands transcends cultural boundaries, but its execution can vary across different societies. In this section, we delve into the captivating world of handshakes in China – a nation steeped in rich tradition and ancient customs.

China, with its long and illustrious history, has its own unique take on the handshake. In Chinese culture, the act of greeting is often accompanied by a slight bow, demonstrating humility and respect. Handshakes are typically reserved for formal occasions or when meeting foreigners. However, it is important to note that handshakes have become increasingly common in business settings due to Western influence.

The Chinese handshake is distinctive in its execution. Unlike the firm grip commonly seen in the West, the Chinese handshake is often gentler and more reserved. It is essential to avoid using excessive force, as this may be seen as aggressive or disrespectful. Maintaining eye contact during the handshake is also highly valued, as it shows sincerity and trustworthiness.

The duration of a Chinese handshake is typically longer than in Western cultures. This extended period of hand clasping symbolizes warmth and genuine interest in the other person. It is essential to be patient and not rush through the gesture, as it may be seen as impolite or insincere.

Additionally, it is worth noting that the Chinese also have certain cultural taboos associated with handshakes. For instance, it is considered impolite to offer a handshake to someone significantly older or of higher social status without receiving an invitation to do so. In such instances, it is advisable to wait for the other person to initiate the handshake.

The Origins of Handshaking in Chinese Culture

The origins of handshaking in Chinese culture can be traced back to ancient times, when it was believed that the handshake symbolized the exchange of energy and the establishment of a spiritual connection between individuals. In traditional Chinese philosophy, the concept of "qi" (pronounced "chee"), or life force energy, played a significant role in interpersonal interactions.

By clasping hands, individuals were believed to be exchanging their personal qi, creating a bond that transcended the physical realm. This exchange was seen to foster understanding, trust, and mutual respect between people.

As Chinese culture evolved, the handshake took on additional meanings and customs. During the Han Dynasty (206 BC – 220 AD), handshakes were used in formal ceremonies and rituals, symbolizing the sealing of agreements and the formation of alliances. The strength and duration of the handshake were considered indicators of the sincerity and commitment of the parties involved.

Handshakes in Modern Chinese Society

In modern Chinese society, handshakes have become increasingly prevalent, particularly in business settings and when interacting with foreigners. However, the traditional Chinese handshake retains its unique characteristics, reflecting the cultural values of modesty, humility, and respect for hierarchy.

One notable aspect of the Chinese handshake is the positioning of the hands. Unlike the Western handshake, where hands are often clasped with palms facing each other, the Chinese handshake typically involves positioning the hands in a vertical orientation, with the palm of one hand facing downward and the other facing upward. This positioning is believed to symbolize the complementary nature of yin and yang, representing balance and harmony in the interaction.

Additionally, the strength and duration of the handshake in Chinese culture are often indicative of the relationship between the individuals involved. A firmer grip and longer duration may signify a closer or more established relationship, while a gentler and shorter handshake may be more appropriate for initial or formal interactions.

Understanding the nuances and intricacies of handshakes in Chinese culture is crucial for forging positive relationships and avoiding potential misunderstandings. By adhering to the customs and traditions associated with Chinese handshakes, one can demonstrate respect and appreciation for the host culture.

Handshakes in China are a fascinating blend of ancient customs and modern influences. The gentle grip, coupled with a slight bow and extended duration, reflects the values of humility, respect, and sincerity. As global interactions become increasingly prevalent, it is essential for individuals to familiarize themselves with the unique customs of each culture, ensuring smooth and harmonious cross-cultural exchanges.

Handshakes in Japan

In the vast tapestry of global cultures, the exchange of greetings is a fundamental aspect of human interaction. Each society has developed its unique way of acknowledging one another, and the handshake has emerged as one of the most common forms of greeting in various parts of the world. In this section, we delve into the intriguing world of handshakes in Japan, exploring their origin, evolution, and cultural significance.

The traditional Japanese greeting, known as "ojigi," involves a deep bow, rather than a handshake. However, in recent times, the influence of Western customs has led to the incorporation of handshakes in Japanese society, particularly in business settings. While the handshake may be perceived as a universal gesture, it is essential to understand the nuances and cultural expectations associated with it in Japan.

The Japanese Handshake

The Japanese handshake is typically lighter and more reserved compared to its Western counterpart. It is usually accompanied by a slight bow, demonstrating respect and humility. The handshake itself is often gentle, with a firm grip but without excessive force. It is crucial to maintain proper eye contact during the interaction, as it demonstrates sincerity and interest.

In Japanese culture, personal space is highly valued, and physical contact is generally less common in everyday interactions. As a result, handshakes are not as prevalent in social situations and are more commonly used in professional settings or when meeting someone for the first time. It is vital to be mindful of this cultural norm to avoid any discomfort or misunderstanding.

It is important to note that the length of a handshake in Japan is typically shorter compared to Western countries. While a firm handshake is appreciated, an extended or overly vigorous handshake may be considered excessive or inappropriate. Adhering to these cultural nuances can help foster positive relationships and prevent unintentional offense.

The Origins and Evolution of Handshakes in Japan

The origins of handshakes in Japan can be traced back to the country's interactions with Western nations during the late 19th century. As Japan opened its doors to the West, diplomatic and trade relations led to the exchange of cultural practices, including the handshake.

Initially, the handshake was viewed with skepticism and even disdain by some traditional Japanese, who saw it as a foreign custom that contradicted the country's cultural norms. However, as Japan modernized and embraced Western influences, the handshake gradually became more accepted, particularly in business and diplomatic circles.

During the early 20th century, the Japanese government actively encouraged the adoption of Western customs, including the handshake, as a means of fostering international relations and projecting a modern image. Japanese businesspeople and diplomats were trained in the proper etiquette of handshaking, and it became a customary practice when interacting with foreign counterparts.

Over time, the handshake evolved and adapted to Japanese cultural sensibilities. While the basic gesture remained, it was often accompanied by a slight bow or nod, reflecting the Japanese emphasis on respect and hierarchy. Additionally, the firmness and duration of the handshake were adjusted to align with Japanese values of modesty and restraint.

Modern Handshake Etiquette in Japan

As Japan continues to engage in global business and cultural exchanges, the handshake has become an integral part of cross-cultural communication. However, it is essential to understand and respect the unique cultural context and etiquette surrounding handshakes in Japan.

In professional settings, such as business meetings or formal events, it is customary to offer a handshake upon initial introductions. The handshake should be firm but not overly forceful, and it is important to maintain eye contact and a respectful demeanor throughout the interaction.

When meeting someone of higher status or seniority, it is advisable to wait for them to initiate the handshake. Additionally, handshakes are typically exchanged between individuals of the same gender, as physical contact between men and women may be seen as inappropriate in certain contexts.

By embracing and respecting these customs, individuals can enhance their understanding of Japanese culture and foster greater harmony and collaboration in an ever-connected world.

Handshakes in India

In the diverse tapestry of cultures around the world, handshakes hold a special place as a universal gesture of greeting and respect. India, with its rich history and deep-rooted traditions, has its own unique customs when it comes to this age-old practice. Exploring the origin and evolution of handshakes in different cultures, it is fascinating to delve into the customs surrounding handshakes in India.

India, known for its warmth and hospitality, regards handshakes as a way to establish trust and build connections. The gesture is not limited to formal settings but is also prevalent in everyday encounters. The Indian handshake is characterized by a gentle grip, often accompanied by a slight bow or nod of the head. This display of respect and humility reflects the values deeply ingrained in Indian society.

The Origins of Handshakes in Indian Culture

The origin of handshakes in India can be traced back to ancient times, where it was believed to symbolize peace and non-violence. In Hindu mythology, Lord Rama, a revered figure, is frequently depicted extending his hand in a gesture of friendship and goodwill. This mythical association has further reinforced the cultural significance of handshakes in India.

Additionally, the handshake finds its roots in the ancient Indian practice of "Namaste," a respectful greeting that involves joining the palms together and bowing slightly. This gesture is believed to stem from the belief that the divine resides within everyone, and the act of joining one's hands signifies the recognition and respect for the divine essence in others.

Regional Variations in Indian Handshakes

Furthermore, the evolution of handshakes in Indian society is evident in the regional variations within the country. In various parts of India, one might encounter unique handshakes that reflect the local customs and traditions.

For instance, in southern India, it is common to see people greet each other by touching their chest with the right hand. This gesture, known as "Namaste," symbolizes respect and is accompanied by a slight bow. In some parts of northern India, people may grasp the other person's hand with both hands, a sign of warmth and affection.

In certain regions, handshakes may also vary based on gender, age, or social status. In more traditional or conservative communities, handshakes between men and women may be limited or avoided altogether, as physical contact between genders is often discouraged.

Handshakes in Modern Indian Society

In recent times, with globalization and the influence of Western cultures, the firm handshake has gained popularity, particularly in business and professional settings. However, it is important to note that the traditional Indian handshake still holds great significance, especially in more traditional and conservative circles.

When engaging in a handshake in India, it is advisable to follow the lead of the other person and adjust the firmness and duration accordingly. A gentle grip and a brief handshake are generally considered respectful and appropriate in most situations.

Furthermore, it is important to be mindful of cultural sensitivities regarding physical contact between genders. In some contexts, it may be appropriate to offer a slight nod or the traditional "Namaste" greeting instead of a handshake, particularly when interacting with individuals of the opposite gender or those from more conservative backgrounds.

The Significance of Handshakes in Indian Culture

The practice of handshakes in India strengthens personal relationships and serves as a bridge between different cultures. It allows individuals to connect on a deeper level, transcending language barriers and cultural differences. Handshakes, in the Indian context, are not merely a formality but a genuine expression of goodwill and camaraderie.

The handshakes in India are deeply rooted in its rich cultural heritage. They signify respect, friendship, and peace, carrying with them a sense of tradition that has evolved over centuries. Whether it is the gentle grip accompanied by a bow or the traditional "Namaste," handshakes in India play a vital role in fostering connections and building relationships in this diverse and vibrant society.

Handshakes in South Asia

In the diverse and culturally rich region of South Asia, handshakes hold significant social and cultural importance. As one delves into the origin and evolution of handshakes in this part of the world, it becomes clear that these gestures are an integral part of the region's social fabric.

South Asia, home to countries such as India, Pakistan, Bangladesh, Nepal, Sri Lanka, and others, boasts a long history of rich traditions and customs. Handshakes in this region have evolved, reflecting the cultural nuances and values of its people.

The Significance of Handshakes in South Asian Cultures

In South Asia, handshakes are not merely perfunctory greetings; they are a way to establish trust, respect, and camaraderie. A firm handshake is considered a sign of sincerity, while a limp one may be seen as a lack of enthusiasm or interest. Additionally, the duration of the handshake is important, with longer handshakes indicating a deeper connection and mutual understanding.

While handshakes are common in many parts of the world, South Asia also has its unique variations. For instance, the 'Namaste' gesture, prevalent in India and Nepal, involves folding hands together and bowing slightly. This gesture, accompanied by a warm smile, demonstrates respect and humility.

Cultural Nuances in South Asian Handshakes

In some South Asian cultures, such as Pakistan and Bangladesh, the right hand is used for handshakes. The left hand is considered impure due to its association with hygiene practices. Therefore, it is essential to be mindful and use the right hand while shaking hands in these countries.

Furthermore, in certain South Asian communities, particularly among conservative Muslims, handshakes between members of the opposite gender may be avoided or limited. This stems from cultural and religious practices that emphasize modesty and preserving personal boundaries.

The Evolution of Handshakes in South Asia

The origins of handshakes in South Asia can be traced back to ancient times when they were used as a symbol of peace and goodwill. In many South Asian cultures, the act of joining hands was seen as a way to establish trust and forge alliances between individuals or tribes.

As civilizations developed and cultures intermingled, the practice of handshaking evolved, taking on different forms and meanings across the region. In some parts of South Asia, handshakes were accompanied by intricate rituals or gestures, reflecting the rich cultural diversity of the region.

With the advent of colonialism and the influence of Western cultures, handshakes became more widespread in South Asia, particularly in urban areas and among the educated elite. However, traditional practices and customs continued to coexist, leading to a unique blend of handshake traditions across the region.

Handshakes in Modern South Asian Societies

In recent times, with globalization and increased cultural exchange, South Asian societies have become more open to adapting to international norms. However, it is crucial to respect and understand the cultural significance of handshakes when interacting with individuals from these regions.

In professional settings and formal occasions, handshakes are widely accepted and practiced in South Asian countries. However, it is advisable to be mindful of the cultural nuances and customs surrounding handshakes, such as the use of the right hand, the duration of the handshake, and the appropriate level of firmness.

Moreover, when interacting with individuals from more traditional or conservative backgrounds, it is important to be respectful of their cultural practices and sensitivities regarding physical contact and gender interactions.

The evolution of handshakes in South Asia reflects the values of respect, trust, and humility that are deeply ingrained in its societies. By understanding and appreciating these customs, individuals from diverse backgrounds can bridge cultural gaps and forge meaningful connections.

Handshakes in South Asia are not very simple greetings; they are symbolic gestures that carry immense cultural significance. As we explore the origin and evolution of handshakes in cultures, it is vital to recognize and respect the customs of South Asia, promoting understanding and appreciation for the rich diversity that exists in our global society.

Chapter 4: Handshakes in Western Cultures

Handshakes in Europe

In the grand tapestry of human communication, few gestures are as universally recognized and practiced as the handshake. This simple act of clasping hands has transcended borders and time, serving as a symbol of trust, respect, and camaraderie. Nowhere is this more evident than in the diverse and fascinating continent of Europe, where handshakes have evolved and taken on unique cultural nuances.

Europe, with its rich history and diverse cultures, is a melting pot of handshake traditions. From the formal and reserved handshakes of the British to the warm and affectionate handshakes of the Italians, each European country has its own distinct style.

Northern Europe

In Northern Europe, a firm, brief handshake is the norm. In countries such as Germany and the Netherlands, a strong grip and direct eye contact demonstrate confidence and professionalism. It is believed that the origins of this firm handshake can be traced back to the Viking age, where a strong grip was seen as a sign of strength and trustworthiness.

However, in Scandinavia, a lighter touch and a more reserved approach are preferred, reflecting their cultural emphasis on personal space and privacy. This tradition is rooted in the region's history, where physical touch was often reserved for close family and friends due to the harsh climate and isolated living conditions.

Western Europe

Moving to Western Europe, we encounter the French, renowned for their elegance and sophistication. In France, handshakes are often accompanied by a light touch on the forearm or a double-cheek kiss, depending on the level of familiarity. This combination of physical contact and warmth reflects their emphasis on building personal connections and stems from the country's rich history of courtly etiquette and social grace.

Eastern Europe

In Eastern Europe, the handshake tradition takes on a more formal and ceremonial tone. In countries like Russia and Ukraine, handshakes are often accompanied by a slight bow or nod of the head, signifying respect, and deference. These gestures are deeply rooted in the region's history and traditional hierarchical structures, influenced by the Byzantine Empire and the Orthodox Christian traditions.

Southern Europe

Southern Europe is known for its vibrant and expressive culture, and this is reflected in their handshakes. In countries like Italy and Spain, handshakes are often accompanied by a warm embrace or a pat on the back. These physical gestures convey a sense of warmth, familiarity, and a desire to establish a personal connection. This tradition can be traced back to the region's Mediterranean roots, where physical touch and affection were valued as expressions of hospitality and friendship.

As we delve into the fascinating world of handshakes in Europe, it becomes clear that this simple gesture is far from uniform. It reflects each country's history, values, and social dynamics. Understanding and appreciating these cultural nuances can help foster better cross-cultural communication and build stronger connections between individuals from diverse backgrounds.

Handshakes in Europe are a testament to the rich diversity of the continent. From the reserved handshakes of Northern Europe to the warm embraces of Southern Europe, each country has its own unique way of expressing trust, respect, and friendship. By exploring and embracing these cultural differences, we can build bridges across cultures and promote a more inclusive and understanding society.

Handshakes in Germany

Germany, known for its rich history and strong cultural traditions, has its own unique customs when it comes to handshakes. This subchapter will explore the origin and evolution of handshakes in German society, shedding light on the significance they hold in this fascinating culture.

The German Handshake Tradition

The handshake, or Hand Druck in German, has been an integral part of German greetings for centuries. It is a symbol of respect, trust, and equality between individuals. In Germany, a firm handshake is preferred, indicating sincerity and confidence. A limp handshake may be interpreted as a lack of interest or insincerity, so it is essential to make a strong impression with a firm grip.

The origins of this emphasis on a firm handshake can be traced back to the medieval era when knights and warriors would grasp each other's hands tightly to signify a binding agreement or alliance. This gesture of strength and trust later became ingrained in German culture as a way of demonstrating one's integrity and commitment.

Furthermore, it is customary to maintain eye contact during a handshake in Germany. This gesture demonstrates respect and shows that you are genuinely interested in the person you are greeting. Avoiding eye contact may be seen as a sign of dishonesty or disinterest, so it is crucial to pay attention to this aspect of the greeting.

Handshakes in German Society

In German society, handshakes are not limited to formal occasions, but are also a widespread practice in casual settings. When meeting someone for the first time, it is customary to shake hands and exchange pleasantries. However, it is essential to note that Germans appreciate punctuality and efficiency. Therefore, it is best to keep the handshake brief and proceed with the conversation promptly.

Another interesting aspect of handshakes in Germany is the hierarchical nature of greetings. When greeting someone of higher social status or authority, it is customary for the subordinate to extend their hand first. This gesture shows deference and respect towards the person of higher rank. Additionally, it is common for Germans to address each other by their last names, using formal titles such as Herr (Mr.) or Frau (Mrs./Ms.).

Handshakes and Cultural Exchange

Recently, due to globalization and the influence of other cultures, alternative forms of greetings such as hugs and kisses on the cheek have become more common in Germany. However, the handshake remains the most widely accepted and respected form of greeting in this society.

Despite the increasing diversity of greetings, the firm handshake remains a deeply ingrained tradition in German culture. It reflects the country's emphasis on professionalism, efficiency, and respect for hierarchies. By understanding and respecting these customs, individuals from diverse backgrounds can navigate social and professional interactions in Germany with greater ease and cultural sensitivity.

In Germany, handshakes are deeply rooted in tradition and signify respect, trust, and equality. Germans value a firm grip, eye contact, and punctuality during greetings. Understanding and respecting these customs are crucial when engaging with German society. So, next time you find yourself in Germany, be sure to offer a firm handshake and make a positive impression.

Handshakes in France

In the grand tapestry of cultural traditions, handshakes serve as a universal symbol of greeting and connection. However, as we delve into the subchapter on Handshakes in France, we uncover a rich history and unique customs surrounding this ubiquitous gesture.

The French Art of Handshaking

France, known for its elegance and sophistication, has its own distinct take on the handshake. It is a country where greetings are highly valued, and the French take considerable pride in their refined mannerisms.

The French handshake is a delicate dance, where technique and timing are of utmost importance. It is typically light, with a gentle squeeze and two or three soft pumps. This subtle yet intentional gesture reflects the French emphasis on maintaining a sense of decorum and respect.

The origins of the French handshake can be traced back to the 17th century when it was commonly used in the royal court and among the aristocracy. During this period, the handshake became a symbol of social grace and etiquette, reflecting the French obsession with refinement and elegance.

The Bise: A Unique Aspect of French Greetings

One interesting aspect of the French handshake is the inclusion of a kiss on both cheeks. In certain regions, such as Paris, Lyon, and Marseille, it is customary to greet acquaintances and friends with la bise, a quick kiss on each cheek. This gesture is a testament to the French emphasis on warmth and intimacy in their social interactions.

The origins of la bise can be traced back to ancient Roman times, when it was a frequent practice to greet friends and family with a kiss on the cheek. This tradition was later adopted by the French and became a part of their cultural identity.

Handshakes in French Society

It is important to note that the French handshake is not limited to formal occasions. In fact, it is a widespread practice among friends, colleagues, and even strangers. A handshake in France is seen as an essential part of establishing trust and building relationships.

In professional settings, the French handshake is often accompanied by a warm smile and direct eye contact. This combination of physical touch and visual engagement is believed to create a sense of rapport and connection between individuals.

Embracing Cultural Differences

Understanding the nuances of handshakes helps bridge the gap between people from diverse backgrounds. By immersing ourselves in the customs of others, we foster a greater appreciation for their traditions and values.

The French handshake is a refined and graceful gesture that reflects the elegance and sophistication of French culture. With its light squeeze and gentle pumps, it serves as a symbol of respect and connection. Combined with the customary kiss on both cheeks, the French handshake represents warmth and intimacy in social interactions. By exploring the origins and evolution of handshakes in various cultures, we gain a more profound understanding of the diverse ways in which human societies connect and communicate.

Handshakes in the United Kingdom

In the vast tapestry of cultural greetings, the handshake stands as a universal symbol of respect, trust, and friendship. Its significance can vary greatly across different cultures, and the United Kingdom is no exception. In this subchapter, we delve into the origin and evolution of handshakes in the United Kingdom, exploring the customs, nuances, and social implications that shape this iconic gesture within British society.

The Medieval Origins of the British Handshake

The roots of the handshake in the UK can be traced back to medieval times, when it was customary for knights to extend their right hand as a sign of peace, ensuring that no weapons were concealed. This gesture was later adopted by the nobility and upper classes to demonstrate their trustworthiness and good intentions.

Over the centuries, this simple act of arm's-length greeting has evolved into a deeply ingrained social convention that transcends class, age, and gender. It became a symbol of respect and a way to establish trust and goodwill between individuals.

The British Handshake Etiquette

While the British handshake is typically brief and formal, it holds tremendous significance in establishing trust and respect. A firm grip and a single up-and-down movement are customary, avoiding excessive force or lingering contact. It is important to maintain eye contact during the handshake, as this demonstrates sincerity and genuine interest in the other person.

However, it is worth noting that the level of firmness and duration of the handshake can vary depending on the social context and the individuals involved. For instance, a more robust handshake may be appropriate in business or professional settings, while a gentler grip might be preferred in more casual or informal situations.

Handshakes and Gender Equality

Interestingly, the British handshake has also adapted to accommodate modern societal changes. In recent years, the rise of gender equality has led to a shift in handshake etiquette. It is now common for women to initiate handshakes, breaking away from the traditional expectation that men must take the lead in this gesture. This is a testament to the evolving dynamics of British society and its commitment to inclusivity.

Handshakes in Professional Settings

In professional settings, the handshake plays a vital role. It is often the first physical contact between business partners or colleagues, and a weak or limp handshake can leave a negative impression. Furthermore, the handshake is an essential component of job interviews and formal introductions, signaling professionalism and integrity.

Employers and interviewers often use the handshake to gauge a candidate's confidence, assertiveness, and overall demeanor. A firm and confident handshake can create a positive first impression and demonstrate a candidate's readiness for the professional world.

Handshakes and British Culture

Beyond its practical applications, the British handshake carries a cultural significance that extends beyond mere formality. It serves as a symbol of unity, cooperation, and trust, fostering a sense of community within British society. The handshake, in its unassuming simplicity, exemplifies the values of respect and equality that the United Kingdom holds dear.

In times of political or social unrest, the act of shaking hands can be a powerful gesture of reconciliation and a willingness to move forward together. It represents a shared commitment to civility, compromise, and the peaceful resolution of conflicts.

The handshake in the United Kingdom has a rich history and has evolved to become an integral part of British culture. From its medieval origins as a gesture of peace to its modern manifestation as a symbol of trust and respect, the British handshake embodies the values and social dynamics of the nation. It serves as a bridge between individuals, fostering connections and building relationships within the diverse tapestry of British society.

Handshakes in North America

Handshakes are an integral part of human interaction, serving as a universal gesture of greeting and respect. However, the way handshakes are conducted can vary significantly across diverse cultures. In this subchapter, we will explore the unique characteristics and evolution of handshakes in North America, shedding light on their significance in this region.

Multicultural Influences

North America is a diverse continent with numerous cultural influences, resulting in a range of handshake customs and practices. While handshakes are generally seen as a formal greeting in North America, subtle variations exist within different countries and even regions. Understanding these nuances can greatly assist individuals in navigating social interactions and forging meaningful connections.

Handshakes in the United States

In the United States, handshakes are considered an important aspect of both personal and professional encounters. A firm handshake, along with direct eye contact and a genuine smile, conveys confidence, trustworthiness, and respect. It is customary to shake hands upon meeting someone for the first time, as well as during business transactions or formal occasions. However, it is significant to note that the level of firmness should be appropriate for the situation – a bone-crushing grip is typically not appreciated!

The origins of the American handshake can be traced back to the country's diverse cultural heritage, drawing influences from European, Native American, and

African traditions. As immigrants from various backgrounds settled in the United States, they brought with them their unique customs and practices, which shaped the modern American handshake.

Handshakes in Canada

Canada, on the other hand, has its own unique handshake customs. Like the United States, a handshake is commonly used as a greeting and signifies respect. However, Canadians tend to have a lighter grip compared to their American counterparts, emphasizing politeness and a non-confrontational approach. In some cases, a gentle touch on the forearm may accompany the handshake as an additional sign of warmth.

The Canadian handshake is also influenced by the country's multiculturalism and the traditions of its diverse population, including indigenous communities, European settlers, and various immigrant groups. This diversity has contributed to the development of a more subdued and inclusive handshake style.

Evolving Trends in North American Handshakes

In recent years, however, there has been a growing trend towards more gender-inclusive greetings in North America. This has resulted in the rise of alternative greetings, such as fist bumps or even hugs, particularly among the younger generation. These gestures aim to create a more relaxed and informal atmosphere while still maintaining a sense of respect and camaraderie.

The COVID-19 pandemic has also had a significant impact on handshake customs in North America. As a precautionary measure to prevent the spread of the virus, many individuals and organizations have embraced alternative greetings, such as elbow bumps or verbal acknowledgments, to maintain social distancing.

Handshakes and Professional Etiquette

In the professional realm, handshakes continue to play a crucial role in North America. A firm and confident handshake is often seen as a positive indicator of an individual's professionalism, assertiveness, and ability to establish rapport. It is a customary practice during job interviews, business meetings, and networking events.

Many companies and organizations provide training on proper handshake etiquette, emphasizing the importance of maintaining eye contact, having a firm grip, and conveying confidence and sincerity through body language.

Respecting Cultural Diversity

The evolution of handshakes in North America reflects the changing social dynamics and cultural values of the region. As society becomes more diverse and interconnected, handshakes adapt to accommodate these shifts. In the face of globalization, it is crucial to be aware of these cultural nuances to effectively communicate and build relationships in a multicultural environment.

Handshakes in North America serve as an important aspect of social and professional interactions. Understanding the customs and variations within different countries and regions can enhance one's ability to connect with individuals from diverse backgrounds. As we delve deeper into the origins and evolution of handshakes across various cultures, we gain a deeper appreciation for the power of this simple yet significant gesture in bridging gaps and fostering unity in our interconnected world.

Handshakes in the United States

In the United States, the handshake is a widely recognized and commonly used form of greeting and parting. It is a gesture that holds great cultural significance and plays a crucial role in American society. Understanding the origin and evolution of handshakes in the United States can provide valuable insights into the country's social fabric and its interactions with other cultures.

The European Roots of the American Handshake

The tradition of handshaking in the United States can be traced back to European customs. Early American settlers brought with them the practice of shaking hands as a sign of trust and goodwill. However, the American handshake has evolved to incorporate its unique characteristics and meanings.

The handshake's significance in American culture can be attributed to the country's diverse population and the blending of various cultural traditions. As immigrants from distinct parts of Europe, Africa, and Asia arrived in the United States, they brought with them a version of their culture.
Here is the continuation of the section on handshakes in the United States with more details added:

The Evolution of the American Handshake

The handshake's significance in American culture can be attributed to the country's diverse population and the blending of various cultural traditions. As immigrants from various parts of Europe, Africa, and Asia arrived in the United States, they brought with them their unique handshaking customs and beliefs.

Over time, these diverse practices began to merge, giving rise to a distinctly American style of handshaking. One of the defining features of the

American handshake is its firmness. A firm grip is often seen as a display of confidence, assertiveness, and sincerity, reflecting the country's emphasis on individualism and self-reliance.

The origins of this firm handshake can be traced back to the early days of the American frontier, where a strong grip was perceived as a sign of physical strength and resilience, qualities that were highly valued in the rugged and untamed wilderness. As the nation expanded westward, this tradition of firm handshakes spread and became ingrained in the American psyche.

Handshake Etiquette in the United States

In the United States, the handshake is a widely recognized and commonly used form of greeting and parting. It is a gesture that holds great cultural significance and plays a crucial role in American society. Understanding the origin and evolution of handshakes in the United States can provide valuable insights into the country's social fabric and its interactions with other cultures.

The tradition of handshaking in the United States can be traced back to European customs. Early American settlers brought with them the practice of shaking hands as a sign of trust and goodwill. However, the American handshake has evolved to incorporate its unique characteristics and meanings.

In the United States, a handshake is typically initiated by extending the right hand with the palm facing upward. The grip is firm but not overly strong, and the handshake lasts for a brief but meaningful duration. Eye contact is also crucial during a handshake, as it signifies sincerity and respect. Breaking eye contact too soon can be seen as a sign of disrespect or lack of interest.

Handshakes in Various Contexts

Handshakes in the United States are not only used in formal settings but are also common in casual interactions. They are frequently exchanged in business meetings, job interviews, and social gatherings. Handshakes are considered a way to establish a personal connection, build trust, and convey mutual respect.

While the basic principles of handshaking remain the same across the United States, there are regional variations that reflect the diverse cultural influences within the country. For example, in the southern states, handshakes tend to be more relaxed and accompanied by a warm smile or even a hug. In contrast, in the northeastern states, handshakes are often more formal and reserved.

The COVID-19 pandemic has brought about significant changes in handshaking customs. With an increased emphasis on personal hygiene and social distancing, many Americans have adopted alternative forms of greetings, such as fist bumps or elbow bumps. However, it is expected that the handshake will regain its prominence as the pandemic subsides and society returns to a sense of normalcy.

Handshakes and Professionalism

In the professional realm, handshakes play a crucial role in establishing credibility and making an impression. A firm and confident handshake is often seen as a positive indicator of an individual's professionalism, assertiveness, and ability to establish rapport.

Many companies and organizations provide training on proper handshake etiquette, emphasizing the importance of maintaining eye contact, having a firm grip, and conveying confidence and sincerity through body language. A weak or limp handshake can be perceived as a lack of confidence or disinterest, potentially hindering professional relationships and opportunities.

Handshakes are also an essential component of job interviews and networking events. A well-executed handshake can create a positive first impression and demonstrate a candidate's readiness for the professional world. Conversely, a poorly executed handshake may cast doubt on an individual's competence and suitability for the role.

Handshakes and American Culture

Handshakes in the United States have a rich history and continue to be an essential part of American culture. They serve as a symbol of trust, respect, and connection. Understanding the origins and evolution of handshakes in the United States provides valuable insights into the country's social dynamics and its interactions with other cultures.

As society evolves and adapts to new circumstances, the handshake will undoubtedly continue to play a significant role in American greetings and interactions. Despite the emergence of alternative greetings, the handshake remains a time-honored tradition that reflects the values of confidence, respect, and mutual understanding that are deeply ingrained in American society.

Navigating Cultural Diversity Through Handshakes

As we delve into the fascinating world of handshakes in Canada, we witness the nation's commitment to multiculturalism, respect, and inclusivity. The handshake serves as a bridge, connecting people from diverse backgrounds and fostering a sense of unity. It is a testament to Canada's rich cultural tapestry and its ever-evolving social fabric.

In Canada, handshakes highlight the country's multicultural heritage, with influences from various traditions. Canadians value firm handshakes, engage in longer durations, and consider handshakes as an essential part of everyday interactions. Moreover, the evolving gender norms have made handshakes more inclusive, reflecting Canada's commitment to equality. Through the simple act of a handshake, Canada embraces its diverse population and fosters connections across cultures.

By understanding and respecting the nuances of handshaking customs in Canada, individuals can navigate cross-cultural interactions with greater ease and sensitivity. This knowledge not only facilitates effective communication but also contributes to building a more inclusive and harmonious society, where diversity is celebrated and embraced.

Chapter 5: Handshakes in African Cultures

Handshakes in West Africa

In the captivating tapestry of human interactions, handshakes have emerged as a universal gesture of greeting and respect. As we delve deeper into the fascinating world of cultural customs, it becomes evident that handshakes have evolved differently in various societies, reflecting their unique values, beliefs, and traditions. In this section, we explore the intriguing realm of handshakes in West Africa, uncovering the origins and evolution of this time-honored tradition.

Handshakes in West Africa are more than mere physical contact; they are symbolic expressions of unity, trust, and goodwill. Rooted in a rich cultural heritage, these handshakes convey a deeper meaning that extends beyond the realm of social niceties. They are a way to establish connections and build relationships, reflecting the communal spirit that characterizes West African societies.

In traditional West African cultures, handshakes are often accompanied by warm smiles and extended eye contact, signifying openness, and acceptance. The gesture is typically performed with the right hand, which holds a significant symbolic value across the region. The right hand is considered purer and more virtuous, reflecting the belief that it is closer to the divine. By extending the right hand in a handshake, individuals demonstrate respect for one another and acknowledge the divine connection that binds them.

Moreover, handshakes in West Africa display the importance of hierarchy and social status. They can vary in intensity and duration depending on the relationship between the individuals involved. When greeting someone of higher status, such as an elder or a tribal leader, a West African handshake may be more elaborate, involving multiple hand movements or even a gentle grasp of the forearm. This gesture emphasizes deference and reverence, highlighting the deep-rooted respect for authority within the culture.

In recent times, with the increasing influence of globalization, Western-style handshakes have become more prevalent in West Africa. However, the traditional customs and cultural nuances remain deeply ingrained in the fabric of society. Handshakes in West Africa have withstood the test of time, adapting to the changing world while still preserving their core values and significance.

As we explore the origins and evolution of handshakes in West Africa, we gain a profound appreciation for the power of this simple yet meaningful gesture. It serves as a reminder that beyond the diversity of cultures, there exists a shared human desire for connection, understanding, and harmony. The handshakes of West Africa, with their inherent warmth and respect, offer us a glimpse into a world where unity and communal bonds are cherished above all.

Handshakes in East Africa

Handshakes have long been recognized as a universal form of greeting, but their significance and mannerisms vary across distinct cultures. In this section, we delve into the intriguing world of handshakes in East Africa, exploring their origin, evolution, and cultural significance.

East Africa, a vibrant region encompassing countries such as Kenya, Tanzania, Uganda, Rwanda, and Ethiopia, is known for its rich diversity of languages, traditions, and customs. Handshakes hold a special place in the social fabric of these nations, serving as a powerful means of communication and connection.

The origins of handshakes in East Africa can be traced back centuries, rooted in the traditional customs and values of the various ethnic groups that inhabit the region. In many communities, a handshake is more than a simple greeting; it symbolizes trust, respect, and goodwill. It is a way to establish a personal connection and build relationships in both formal and informal settings.

One of the fascinating aspects of handshakes in East Africa is the diversity of styles and gestures employed. In some communities, a handshake is accompanied by a gentle grip and a slight bow, demonstrating humility and deference. In others, handshakes are more vigorous, involving multiple shakes and even shoulder bumps, signifying enthusiasm, and warmth.

The gender dynamics associated with handshakes in East Africa are worth exploring. In certain cultures, it is customary for men to shake hands with each other as well as with women. However, in more conservative societies, men may refrain from shaking hands with women to respect cultural norms and gender boundaries.

To hugely appreciate the significance of handshakes in East Africa, it is essential to understand the cultural context in which they are practiced. Handshakes often accompany important rituals and ceremonies, such as weddings, funerals, and business negotiations. They can also be used to seal agreements, mend disputes, and express condolences.

In recent years, the rapid globalization and influence of Western culture have led to a blending of traditions in East Africa. While the handshake remains a prominent form of greeting, it is common to see elements of Western styles incorporated, such as a firm grip and eye contact.

As we immerse ourselves in the diverse cultures of East Africa, we come to appreciate the profound role handshakes play in fostering relationships, bridging gaps, and promoting unity. Through this exploration, we gain a deeper understanding of the evolution of handshakes in diverse cultures, shedding light on the remarkable ways in which societies connect and communicate across borders.

Handshakes in East Africa reflect the region's cultural richness and diversity. From their origins rooted in tradition to their evolving styles and gestures, handshakes serve as a powerful tool for communication, respect, and building meaningful connections. By embracing and understanding the nuances of handshakes in East Africa, we can deeply appreciate the beauty of cross-cultural interactions and the universal language of human connection.

Handshakes in Southern Africa

In the vast and diverse continent of Africa, the practice of handshaking takes on unique meanings and customs in every region. Southern Africa, with its rich cultural heritage and vibrant societies, is no exception. Handshakes in this part of the continent are not merely a form of greeting; they reflect the values and traditions deeply ingrained in the local communities.

Southern Africa is home to numerous ethnic groups, each with their distinct customs and protocols.

Handshakes serve as a means of showing respect, establishing trust, and fostering social bonds among individuals. The people of Southern Africa view handshakes as an opportunity to connect on a personal level and build relationships that extend beyond simple courtesy.

One common handshake tradition in Southern Africa is the use of both hands during the greeting. This gesture is seen as a sign of sincerity and warmth, indicating that the person offering the handshake is genuinely interested in establishing a connection. It also serves to convey equality and balance between two individuals, emphasizing the importance of mutual respect and understanding.

Another prominent feature of handshakes in Southern Africa is the duration of the gesture. Unlike the quick and brief handshakes commonly seen in other cultures, handshakes here can be more prolonged, lasting several seconds. This extended duration allows individuals to engage in conversation, exchange pleasantries, and demonstrate their genuine interest in one another.

Handshakes in Southern Africa often incorporate other forms of non-verbal communication. A gentle touch on the forearm or shoulder, combined with a handshake, can convey empathy, compassion, and a sense of solidarity. These subtle gestures are deeply rooted in the local culture, reflecting the importance placed on forming meaningful connections and offering support to others.

The evolution of handshakes in Southern Africa is closely tied to the region's history of colonization, migration, and cultural exchange. Over time, these interactions have influenced and shaped the local customs surrounding handshakes. Today, handshakes in Southern Africa serve not only as a means of greeting but also as a symbol of unity, respect, and cultural identity.

Handshakes in Southern Africa are a fascinating reflection of the region's diverse cultures and traditions. From the use of both hands to the extended duration and incorporation of non-verbal gestures, the handshakes in this part of the continent are a testament to the importance of personal connections and mutual respect. As we explore the origin and

evolution of handshakes in different cultures, it is
essential to appreciate and understand the unique
customs and values that underpin these gestures in
Southern Africa.

Chapter 6: Handshakes in Indigenous Cultures

Handshakes in Native American Cultures

The origin and evolution of handshakes in diverse
cultures have always fascinated society. It is through
these simple gestures that we can understand the rich
history and cultural diversity of various civilizations. In
this section, we delve into the world of Native
American cultures and explore the significance of
handshakes in their traditions.

Native American cultures have a deep-rooted
connection with nature and a profound respect for
their surroundings. Handshakes in their societies were
not merely greetings but held profound symbolic
meanings. These gestures were seen to establish trust,
foster unity, and communicate nonverbally.

In many Native American tribes, the handshake was performed with both hands, which symbolized the coming together of two individuals or two tribes. This gesture represented the sharing of energy and information, emphasizing equality and mutual respect. It was a way to honor the sacred bond between individuals and acknowledge the interconnectedness of all living beings.

Different tribes had their unique variations of handshakes. For instance, the Lakota Sioux tribe would extend their right hand while touching the left arm of the other person, signifying sincerity, and friendship. The Apache tribe, on the other hand, would perform a more vigorous handshake to convey strength and vigor.

In addition to their symbolic significance, handshakes in Native American cultures were also used as a form of introduction and acknowledgment. When meeting a new person or entering someone's home, it was customary to offer a handshake to show respect and establish a positive rapport.

The arrival of European settlers and the subsequent colonization of Native American lands brought about significant changes in their cultures, including their traditional greetings. The introduction of European customs, such as the single-handed handshake, gradually replaced the traditional Native American handshakes. However, many tribes continue to preserve their unique greetings and pass them down through generations.

Understanding the history and evolution of handshakes in Native American cultures allows us to appreciate the depth and diversity of human interactions. Through these gestures, we can unravel the stories of ancient civilizations and their profound connections to the natural world. So, the next time you extend your hand for a handshake, remember the rich traditions and legacies that have shaped this simple act.

Handshakes in Aboriginal Cultures

In the vast tapestry of cultural practices and traditions, the handshake holds a special place as a universal greeting gesture. As we explore the origin and evolution of handshakes in different cultures, it is crucial to delve into the unique customs and significance they hold in Aboriginal cultures.

Aboriginal cultures, representing the indigenous peoples of various regions, have a rich history that predates the arrival of European settlers. With diverse languages, customs, and beliefs, these cultures have developed their own distinct ways of greeting and connecting with others.

In Aboriginal cultures, the handshake is more than just a simple physical gesture; it serves as a bridge between individuals, communities, and even spirits. The act of shaking hands signifies trust, respect, and a willingness to engage in a meaningful exchange. It is a way of acknowledging the presence and importance of the other person or group.

In some Aboriginal cultures, handshakes are performed with both hands, emphasizing the value placed on the connection being made. This double-handed handshake signifies the coming together of two individuals or communities, mutually acknowledging their shared history, experiences, and aspirations. It is a powerful symbol of unity and solidarity.

The handshake also plays a significant role in Aboriginal ceremonies and rituals. It is often used to establish a spiritual connection with ancestors or to seek blessings from the land and its natural forces. Elders and community leaders, who hold immense wisdom and authority, often initiate handshakes during these sacred gatherings, passing on their blessings and knowledge to those they greet.

The handshake serves as a means of communication within Aboriginal cultures. It can convey messages of friendship, gratitude, and even apology. Each handshake is unique, reflecting the specific context and relationship between the individuals involved.

In today's multicultural society, the Aboriginal handshake continues to be a powerful symbol of cultural identity and a way to forge connections between diverse communities. It reminds us of the importance of respecting and embracing different cultural practices, fostering understanding and appreciation for one another.

As we explore the evolution of handshakes across cultures, it is essential to recognize the significance and beauty of Aboriginal traditions. The handshake in Aboriginal cultures embodies the values of trust, respect, unity, and spirituality, serving as a reminder of the rich tapestry of human connections that shape our world.

Handshakes in Maori Culture

In the vast tapestry of global customs and traditions, the Maori people of New Zealand have woven a unique and captivating culture. A significant aspect of Maori customs is the art of communication, which includes their distinctive approach to handshakes. Exploring the handshakes in Maori culture provides us with a fascinating glimpse into the rich heritage and intricate social dynamics of this indigenous community.

The Maori people view handshakes as a sacred ritual, a physical expression of respect, unity, and trust. Known as the "hongi," this traditional greeting involves pressing one's nose and forehead against the other person's, symbolizing the exchange of breath and the merging of life forces. While this may seem unfamiliar to those outside of Maori culture, it is a powerful gesture that establishes a deep connection between individuals.

The hongi holds profound significance in Maori society, as it is not solely a form of greeting but also a way to acknowledge one's ancestors and express gratitude for the land. It is a customary practice at the beginning of important gatherings, such as weddings, funerals, or official meetings. By sharing breath, the Maori believe they are connecting with the spiritual essence of their ancestors and the natural world around them.

Unlike the Western handshake, the hongi does not rely on physical strength or firmness of grip. Instead, it emphasizes the connection of spirits and the building of relationships. It is a gentle and intimate gesture, requiring both parties to approach with an open heart and mind. Through the hongi, the Maori people communicate their values of inclusivity, humility, and interconnectedness.

Understanding the hongi provides a valuable insight into the evolution of handshakes in distinct cultures.

While some cultures prioritize formality and assertiveness, the Maori focus on unity and spiritual connection. The hongi is a testament to the Maori people's deep-rooted connection to their land and ancestors, a connection that is vital to their sense of identity and community.

Handshakes in Maori culture is far more than a simple greeting; they are a way of connecting with one's heritage, ancestors, and the natural world. The hongi serves as a symbol of respect, unity, and trust, reflecting the values of the Maori people. By exploring the unique handshakes in depth, we gain a greater understanding of the diverse ways in which societies communicate and build relationships. The hongi is a testament to the beauty and depth of Maori culture, reminding us of the importance of acknowledging our shared humanity and interconnectedness across cultures.

Chapter 7: Modern Adaptations and Variations of Handshakes

Handshake Etiquette in Business Settings

In our globalized world, where businesses operate across borders and cultures, understanding and respecting the customs and traditions of different societies is crucial. One such custom that holds immense significance in various cultures is the handshake. It is a universal gesture of greeting and establishing trust, and its proper execution is vital in business settings. In this section, we will explore the etiquette of handshakes in various cultures and how it has evolved.

The practice of handshakes can be traced back to ancient times, where it played a fundamental role as a symbol of peace and goodwill among individuals. Nevertheless, its significance has evolved and extended far beyond its initial purpose of mere greetings. In various cultures worldwide, the handshake holds diverse and profound meanings, intricately intertwined with subtle nuances that must be wholeheartedly acknowledged and respected in the realm of business interactions and beyond.

For instance, in Western cultures such as the United States and Europe, a firm handshake is seen as a sign of confidence, trustworthiness, and professionalism.

However, in Middle Eastern cultures, a gentle handshake with a slight bow is more appropriate, highlighting respect and humility. Similarly, in Asian cultures, such as Japan and China, a slight bow with a light handshake is customary, emphasizing politeness and maintaining harmony. Understanding these cultural variations is essential to avoid misunderstandings and build strong business relationships.

The evolution of handshakes in society has led to the emergence of new norms. With the COVID-19 pandemic, the traditional handshake has come under scrutiny due to health concerns. As a result, alternative greetings like elbow bumps or namaste (a traditional Hindu gesture) have gained popularity. Navigating these changes while respecting cultural norms requires adaptability and sensitivity.

In business settings, mastering handshake etiquette is crucial to project professionalism and create positive impressions. It is essential to make eye contact, offer a firm (but not overpowering) grip, and maintain an appropriate duration. Additionally, being aware of local customs, such as the use of the left hand or the acceptance of business cards with both hands, can elevate your credibility and demonstrate cultural intelligence.

Handshakes have evolved from simple greetings to complex gestures with cultural significance in business settings. Understanding the origins, customs, and etiquette associated with handshakes in distinct cultures is vital for successful cross-cultural communication. By respecting these traditions and adapting to changes, we can bridge the gaps between societies and foster meaningful connections, enhancing business opportunities on a global scale.

What the Handshake Means and How Trusting Is a Handshake

In the intriguing and captivating realm of cross-cultural interactions, the handshake has truly emerged as a universally recognized and respected gesture, embodying profound meanings of greeting and respect. It serves as a powerful symbol of trust, goodwill, and mutual understanding, transcending even the most formidable language barriers and cultural disparities. This section embarks on a comprehensive exploration of the immense significance that lies behind the act of shaking hands, shedding light on the multifaceted dimensions of trust it represents across diverse cultures and societies.

The history of the handshake is an extraordinary and rich tapestry that spans countless centuries. Tracing its origins back to ancient civilizations such as Egypt and Greece, this iconic gesture was initially employed to convey the peaceful intentions of an individual, highlighting their unarmed status and fostering an atmosphere of trust and sincerity. As the sands of time continued to shift, the handshake gradually transformed into an ingrained customary greeting, serving as an instrument to forge connections and cultivate harmonious relationships.

However, it is crucial to recognize that the meaning and significance of the handshake can differ across cultures. In some societies, a firm grip and strong handshake are seen as signs of strength and confidence. In others, a gentle and lingering handshake is preferred, emphasizing warmth and intimacy. Understanding these cultural nuances is essential to avoiding misinterpretation and fostering positive cross-cultural relationships.

Moreover, the level of trust associated with a handshake can also vary. In some cultures, a handshake is seen as a binding agreement, a commitment to honor one's word. This level of trust is deeply ingrained and carries immense weight. In contrast, in other cultures, the handshake may be seen as a mere formality, a polite gesture devoid of any real meaning. Recognizing these disparities is crucial when engaging in international business or diplomatic negotiations.

It is fascinating to delve into the evolution of handshakes across diverse cultures. For example, in Japan, a slight bow accompanies the handshake, demonstrating respect and humility. In Middle Eastern cultures, handshakes are often prolonged, with frequent pauses for conversation, reflecting the value placed on personal relationships and social connections.

Navigating the intricacies of handshakes requires an open mind, cultural sensitivity, and a willingness to learn from others. By understanding the meaning behind a handshake and the varying degrees of trust it represents, we can bridge cultural gaps and build meaningful connections with people from diverse backgrounds.

The handshake is a powerful symbol that transcends borders and unifies humanity. From its humble beginnings as a gesture of peace to its modern-day role as a universal greeting, the handshake embodies trust, respect, and understanding. However, it is important to remember that its interpretation and significance can vary significantly across cultures. By embracing these differences and adapting our approach, we can ensure that the handshake remains a meaningful and inclusive gesture in our increasingly interconnected world.

Chapter 7: How Business Can Be Done on a Handshake

An Age-Old Tradition

In a world driven by contracts and legal agreements, the idea of conducting business on a simple handshake may seem archaic or even risky. However, the practice of sealing deals with a firm grip and eye contact has deep roots in various cultures around the world. This section explores how business can be conducted successfully with a handshake, considering the origin and evolution of handshakes.

Throughout history, handshakes have served as a universal symbol of trust, respect, and mutual understanding. The act of extending one's hand towards another is a gesture that transcends language barriers and cultural differences, exemplifying a profound willingness to engage and collaborate. This timeless tradition forms an ideal foundation for business dealings, fostering a sense of unity and cooperation.

In various cultures around the world, particularly in Western societies, handshakes have become synonymous with business transactions, embodying a formal agreement that extends beyond mere words. It is a binding contract that is not confined to paper but rather etched in the very integrity of those involved. The firmness of the grip, the duration of the handshake, and the unwavering eye contact all convey crucial messages about one's character, intentions, and commitment to the accord at hand. Such subtle nuances further emphasize the depth and significance of this revered custom.

In other cultures, handshakes may be accompanied by additional gestures or rituals. For example, in Japan, a bow may follow a handshake, demonstrating respect and humility. In the Middle East, handshakes are often preceded by inquiries about one's well-being and family, reflecting the importance of building personal relationships before engaging in business negotiations.

The beauty of conducting business by a handshake lies in its simplicity and authenticity. It encourages open communication and promotes a sense of equality between parties. It implies a willingness to fulfill commitments and a belief in the power of one's word. In a world where legal jargon and contracts can sometimes overshadow human connections, the handshake reminds us of the importance of trust and personal relationships in business.

Conducting business on a handshake does not mean disregarding legal safeguards entirely. It is essential to strike a balance between trust and prudence. However, by incorporating elements of the handshake tradition into our modern business practices, we can foster stronger relationships, enhance collaboration, and create a more inclusive and compassionate business environment.

The practice of conducting business on a handshake has endured throughout history for a reason. It transcends cultural boundaries and serves as a universal symbol of trust. By understanding the origin and evolution of handshakes, we can appreciate the power of this age-old tradition and its potential to reshape the way we do business today. So, let us extend our hands, make eye contact, and embrace the spirit of trust and collaboration that the handshake represents.

Handshakes in Social Interactions

The origin and evolution of handshakes have played a significant role in shaping societal norms and facilitating human connections. From ancient customs to modern-day greetings, the handshake remains a universal gesture that transcends boundaries and fosters mutual understanding. In this section, we will explore the rich history and cultural significance of handshakes, delving into their origins, variations, and symbolism across different societies.

Handshakes have deep roots in human history, with evidence of their existence found in ancient cave paintings and archaeological artifacts. Throughout the ages, handshakes have evolved from simple gestures of friendship to complex rituals with profound cultural meanings. From the firm grip of Western societies to the gentle grasp of Eastern cultures, the way handshakes are executed varies, reflecting the diversity of human interactions.

In many cultures, handshakes serve multiple purposes beyond a mere greeting. They can convey respect, trust, and acceptance, making them vital in establishing social connections. For instance, in some African tribes, handshakes are accompanied by intricate hand movements and finger snaps, symbolizing unity and shared values. In contrast, the traditional Maori hongi, a gentle pressing of noses and foreheads, signifies the exchange of breath and the merging of spirits.

Furthermore, handshakes often carry gender-specific or hierarchical connotations. In certain societies, women might greet each other with a softer handshake, while men engage in firmer and more assertive handshakes. Similarly, handshakes between individuals of different social statuses may vary in intensity and duration, reflecting power dynamics and social hierarchies.

Understanding the cultural nuances of handshakes is crucial in navigating social interactions and building bridges across cultures. Misunderstandings or misinterpretations of handshake customs can lead to unintended offense or confusion. By appreciating the diversity of handshakes and their cultural significance, we can build stronger connections and foster inclusivity within our global society.

Handshakes have played a pivotal role in the evolution of social interactions across cultures. Their origins can be traced back to ancient times, and they have since evolved into intricate gestures laden with cultural meanings. By exploring the spectrum of handshakes in various societies, we gain a deeper understanding of the diverse ways humans connect and communicate.

As we continue to interact with individuals from divergent backgrounds, a comprehensive understanding of handshakes can help bridge cultural gaps and promote harmony in our ever-evolving global society.

Handshakes in Sports and Entertainment

In the realm of sports and entertainment, handshakes have always played a significant role. They have become a universal gesture that transcends cultural boundaries, symbolizing respect, sportsmanship, and camaraderie. This section explores the origin and evolution of handshakes in different cultures within these domains, shedding light on the power of this simple yet profound act.

Sports, as a platform for competition and collaboration, have embraced handshakes as a symbol of fair play. From ancient Olympic Games to modern-day sporting events, athletes have used handshakes to express their respect for opponents, regardless of the outcome. In this context, handshakes serve as a reminder that sports are not just about victory and defeat but also about mutual respect and admiration for one another's skills and efforts.

Various sports have developed their unique handshake traditions. For instance, in basketball, players often engage in a pre-game handshake routine, forming a bond before the intense competition begins. In tennis, players shake hands at the net after a match, acknowledging each other's efforts and displaying good sportsmanship. Handshakes have become an integral part of sports culture, reinforcing the values of fairness, unity, and respect.

Similarly, in the world of entertainment, handshakes hold great significance. Actors, musicians, and performers often greet each other with handshakes before taking the stage or engaging in collaborative endeavors. These handshakes act as a symbol of trust and camaraderie, setting the stage for successful collaborations and memorable performances.

Handshakes in entertainment have evolved to include unique variations, such as the "fist bump" or the "high five." These gestures signify solidarity and support and create a sense of connection between performers and their audiences. Handshakes have become a way for entertainers to bridge the gap between themselves and their fans, creating a shared experience that transcends cultural and societal boundaries.

The evolution of handshakes in sports and entertainment mirrors the broader societal changes and cultural shifts. It demonstrates the power of a universal gesture to foster unity, respect, and understanding among individuals from diverse backgrounds. As sports and entertainment continue to evolve, handshakes will undoubtedly maintain their significance, reminding us of the values that bind us together as a society.

Handshakes in sports and entertainment serve as powerful symbols of respect, sportsmanship, and collaboration. They transcend cultural boundaries, evolving to represent the values of fairness, unity, and camaraderie. From pre-game rituals to post-performance acknowledgments, handshakes have become an integral part of these domains, creating connections that go beyond language and nationality. As we explore the origin and evolution of handshakes in distinct cultures within sports and entertainment, we gain a deeper appreciation for the universal language of respect and unity that they represent.

Chapter 8: The Future of Handshakes and Cultural Exchange

The Impact of Technology on Handshake Traditions

Technology has revolutionized every aspect of our lives, including the way we interact and communicate. One of the areas that has been significantly affected by technology is the age-old tradition of handshakes. In this section, we will explore the profound impact that technology has had on handshake traditions and its implications for society.

Handshakes have long served as a universal symbol of trust, respect, and greeting in cultures around the world. They have been a crucial part of our social fabric, allowing us to establish connections and build relationships. However, with the advent of technology, the traditional handshake is facing new challenges and transformations.

Virtual Communication and the Erosion of Physical Touch

One of the most evident impacts of technology on handshake traditions is the rise of virtual communication. With the increasing reliance on video conferences, emails, and social media platforms, virtual alternatives have replaced physical handshakes. While these alternatives may offer convenience and efficiency, they lack the individualized touch and physical presence that a handshake provides. As a result, the sense of trust and connection that a handshake fosters are often diminished in virtual interactions.

Skepticism and Distrust in the Digital Age

Furthermore, technology has also influenced the way we perceive and interpret handshakes. In the digital age, images and videos can be easily manipulated, leading to a rise in skepticism and distrust. This skepticism extends to handshakes as well, with people questioning the authenticity and intentions behind a handshake captured on camera. The age-old belief that a firm handshake is a sign of integrity and confidence may no longer hold the same weight in the digital realm.

The Rise of Touch-less Technologies

Moreover, the rise of touch-less technologies, such as contactless payment systems and biometric authentication, has further reduced the need for physical contact, including handshakes. These technologies offer convenience and hygiene benefits, but they also contribute to the erosion of the traditional handshake ritual.

Preserving the Value of Physical Interactions

As technology continues to advance, it is imperative for society to reflect on the impact it has on our cultural traditions. While handshakes may evolve or even fade away in the face of technological advancements, it is important to recognize the significance of physical contact and personal interactions in fostering trust and building relationships. As we navigate the digital age, we must find a balance between embracing the benefits of technology and preserving the fundamental values that handshakes represent in our diverse cultures.

The impact of technology on handshake traditions cannot be ignored. Virtual communication, skepticism towards digital handshakes, and touch-less technologies have reshaped the way we greet and establish connections. However, it is crucial for society to reflect on the importance of physical contact and personal interactions, as they play a vital role in building trust and understanding between individuals. As we continue to adapt to the digital age, it is essential to find a balance between embracing technology and preserving the cultural significance of handshakes.

Globalization and the Homogenization of Handshake Practices

The phenomenon of globalization has led to an increasing interchange of ideas, cultures, and practices across borders. As the world becomes more interconnected, one aspect that has seen notable change is the way people greet each other. Handshakes, a universal symbol of goodwill and trust, have evolved over centuries in diverse cultures,

reflecting unique customs, beliefs, and values.
However, with the rise of globalization, there has been
a growing concern about the homogenization of
handshake practices.

The origin and evolution of handshakes in diverse
cultures is a fascinating subject that sheds light on the
diversity of human interactions. From the firm and
assertive handshakes of Western cultures to the gentle
and lingering handshakes of East Asia, each culture has
developed its own unique style, often influenced by
historical, social, and religious factors. The book " The
Handshake "Around the World " delves into the rich
tapestry of handshake practices, offering readers an
opportunity to explore the origins and meanings
behind these gestures.

However, as the world becomes increasingly
interconnected, there is a growing concern that
globalization is leading to the homogenization of
handshake practices. With the rise of multinational
corporations, international diplomacy, and global
travel, there is a tendency for people to adopt a
standardized approach to handshaking, often
influenced by Western norms. This can lead to a loss of

cultural diversity and the erosion of traditional customs.

While globalization has undoubtedly contributed to the spread of Western-style handshakes, it is important to recognize the value of cultural diversity in greetings. Handshakes are not merely formalities; they are windows into a culture's history, values, and social norms. By understanding and respecting the unique handshake practices, we can foster greater intercultural understanding and appreciation.

"Globalization and the Homogenization of Handshake Practices" delves into the impact of globalization on the diverse world of handshakes. The Evolution of Handshakes in Society" aims to raise awareness about the importance of preserving cultural diversity in greetings. In an increasingly interconnected world, it is crucial to recognize and respect the unique customs and practices that shape our interactions, and handshakes serve as a tangible reminder of our shared humanity and the richness of our global tapestry.

The Role of Handshakes in Promoting Intercultural Understanding

Handshakes have long been a universal form of greeting and establishing rapport between individuals. In today's globalized world, where intercultural interactions are becoming increasingly common, understanding the significance and variations of handshakes across cultures is crucial. This section aims to explore the role of handshakes in promoting intercultural understanding, shedding light on the origin and evolution of handshakes.

Handshakes serve as a powerful non-verbal communication tool, transcending language barriers and conveying respect, trust, and goodwill. They provide a unique opportunity to establish a connection and bridge cultural divides. By studying the origin and evolution of handshakes in diverse cultures, we can gain insights into the values and customs that underpin these gestures.

In some cultures, the firmness of a handshake is seen as an indicator of one's character and strength. For instance, in Western societies, a firm handshake is considered a sign of confidence and trustworthiness. However, in other cultures, a strong grip may be interpreted as aggressive or disrespectful. Understanding these nuances is crucial in avoiding unintended offense or miscommunication when engaging with individuals from diverse backgrounds.

Handshakes vary in duration, hand positioning, and even the use of the left or right hand. For example, in many Middle Eastern cultures, the right hand is considered clean and appropriate for handshakes, while the left hand is associated with personal hygiene and considered unclean. By understanding these cultural differences, we can navigate social interactions respectfully and promote intercultural understanding.

The evolution of handshakes in society can also reveal fascinating insights into historical and societal changes. For instance, in ancient Rome, handshakes were used to check for concealed weapons, reflecting a time of heightened warfare and mistrust. In contrast, the Maori people of New Zealand engage in the hongi, a traditional greeting where individuals press their noses together, symbolizing the sharing of the breath of life. By exploring these cultural practices, we can gain a deeper appreciation for the diversity of human expression and the ways in which societies have adapted over time.

Handshakes play a vital role in promoting intercultural understanding. By understanding the origin and evolution of handshakes in distinct cultures, we can navigate cross-cultural interactions with sensitivity and respect. Handshakes serve as a universal language of connection and can help bridge cultural divides, building trust and fostering meaningful relationships. In an increasingly interconnected world, the study of handshakes is an essential tool for fostering a more inclusive and understanding society.

The Continuing Significance of Handshakes in a Diverse Society

In this book, " The Handshake "Around the World," we have explored the fascinating origin and evolution of handshakes in different cultures. From ancient civilizations to modern-day societies, the handshake has served as a universal gesture of greeting, respect, and trust. As we conclude this journey, it becomes evident that handshakes hold a continuing significance in our diverse society.

Throughout history, handshakes have played a crucial role in fostering connections and building relationships. The act of extending one's hand in greeting transcends language barriers and cultural differences. It is a simple yet powerful gesture that communicates openness, acceptance, and goodwill. Handshakes can bridge gaps and bring people together, regardless of their backgrounds.

In a diverse society, where individuals from various cultures interact, the handshake becomes even more significant. It serves as a symbol of unity and understanding, promoting harmony and cooperation. By engaging in this age-old tradition, we acknowledge and honor the customs and traditions of others. Handshakes allow us to embrace diversity and celebrate the richness of our multicultural world.

Moreover, handshakes convey respect and trust. When we offer a hand to someone, we invite them into our personal space, demonstrating our willingness to connect on a deeper level. This physical contact establishes a sense of familiarity and creates a foundation for meaningful interactions. Handshakes create a sense of mutual respect, signaling our commitment to treat each other as equals.

In today's digital age, where virtual communication has become the norm, the significance of handshakes may seem diminished. However, this physical gesture remains irreplaceable. In an era of social distancing, it is essential to recognize the importance of personal connections. Handshakes remind us of our shared humanity and the need for physical interaction in an increasingly disconnected world.

As we move forward in our diverse society, let us not forget the profound significance of handshakes. Let us continue to embrace this universal gesture, respecting and valuing the customs and traditions. By extending our hands in friendship, we can bridge cultural divides, foster understanding, and promote a more inclusive society.

Handshakes are not merely a historical relic but an enduring symbol of unity, respect, and trust. They serve as a reminder of our shared humanity and our ability to connect across cultural boundaries. Let us continue to use the handshake as a tool for building relationships and fostering a more inclusive and harmonious society.

www.ingramcontent.com/pod-product-compliance
Lightning Source LLC
LaVergne TN
LVHW010636200726

843507LV00011B/1707